Squaring the Circles:
The Reach of Colonial America

AMERICAN HISTORY NOW

Series edited by Eric Foner and Lisa McGirr

Other titles in the series:

AMERICAN REVOLUTION AND EARLY REPUBLIC
■ Woody Holton

JACKSONIAN AMERICA
■ Seth Rockman

SLAVERY, THE CIVIL WAR, AND RECONSTRUCTION
■ Adam Rothman

THE POSSIBILITIES OF POLITICS: DEMOCRACY IN AMERICA, 1877 TO 1917
■ Robert D. Johnston

THE INTERWAR YEARS
■ Lisa McGirr

THE UNCERTAIN FUTURE OF AMERICAN POLITICS, 1940 TO 1973
■ Meg Jacobs

1973 TO THE PRESENT
■ Kim Phillips-Fein

THE UNITED STATES IN THE WORLD
■ Erez Manela

THE "CULTURAL TURN"
■ Lawrence B. Glickman

AMERICAN RELGION
■ John T. McGreevy

FRONTIERS, BORDERLANDS, WESTS
■ Stephen Aron

ENVIRONMENTAL HISTORY
■ Sarah T. Phillips

HISTORY OF AMERICAN CAPITALISM
■ Sven Beckert

WOMEN'S AND GENDER HISTORY
■ Rebecca Edwards

IMMIGRATION AND ETHNIC HISTORY
■ Mae M. Ngai

AMERICAN INDIANS AND THE STUDY OF U.S. HISTORY
■ Ned Blackhawk

AFRICAN-AMERICAN HISTORY
■ Kevin Gaines

To purchase these and other titles,
visit the American Historical Association's online store at

www.historians.org/pubshop

American History Now

Squaring the Circles:
The Reach of Colonial America

By

Alan Taylor

With a foreword by **Eric Foner** and **Lisa McGirr**, series editors

American Historical Association
400 A Street, SE
Washington, DC 20003
www.historians.org

ALAN TAYLOR is professor of history at the University of California at Davis, and the author of *William Cooper's Town: Power and Persuasion on the Frontier of the Early American Republic* (1996), which won the Pulitzer Prize for American History. His most recent book is *The Civil War of 1812: American Citizens, British Subjects, Indian Allies and Irish Rebels* (2010).

COVER DESIGN AND LAYOUT: Chris Hale

Published in 2012 by the American Historical Association. As publisher, the American Historical Association does not adopt official views on any field of history and does not necessarily agree or disagree with the views expressed in this book.

This essay originally appeared in *American History Now* (ISBN 978-1-4399-0243-1), published by Temple University Press as part of the series Critical Perspectives on the Past, edited by Susan Porter Benson, Stephen Brier, and the late Roy Rosenzweig.

Library of Congress Cataloging-in-Publication data:

Taylor, Alan, 1955–

Squaring the circles : the reach of colonial America / by Alan Taylor; with a foreword by Eric Foner and Lisa McGirr.

p. cm. — (American history now)

ISBN 978-0-87229-181-2

1. United States—History—Colonial period, ca. 1600–1775—Historiography. I. Title.

E188.T355 2012

973.2—dc23   2012018627

Table of Contents

Series Foreword

First published in 1990, followed by a revised and expanded edition seven years later, *The New American History* introduced a generation of students, teachers, and members of the broader public to the ongoing transformation of the study of the American past. In the early twenty-first century, that transformation has continued apace. In embarking on a third edition, the editors decided to assemble an entirely new collection. First, we expanded the number of essays to eighteen, to allow us to incorporate emerging subfields not represented in the original editions. Second, we invited an entirely new group of historians to contribute. Each of the essays that follow is written by a young scholar at the forefront of current trends in his or her area of expertise. Eight deal with a specific time period, beginning with the colonial era; the remainder assess recent developments in historians' understanding of a major theme in the nation's past. To signal these substantive and generational changes, we gave the volume the new title *American History Now*.

It is worth noting at the outset that we have made no attempt to impose a uniform outlook or single interpretation on the contributors. We have given each author a free hand in defining his or her subject and developing an approach to it. Inevitably, therefore, there are overlaps, especially between chronological and thematic essays, as well as differences in emphasis and outlook. Nonetheless, certain themes recur with remarkable regularity.

The first editions of *The New American History* demonstrated, above all, the impact of the "new social history" on our understanding of the American past. Inspired initially by the social movements of the 1960s and 1970s, and influenced by methods and insights borrowed from other disciplines and from scholars of other national histories, American historians redefined the cast of characters who made up the nation's past. They devoted their energies to recovering the experience of previously neglected groups, not simply as an addition to a preexisting body of knowledge but as a fundamental redefinition of history itself. In the wake of that explosion of scholarship, our understanding of American history past was enormously enriched and expanded.

The scholars in this new edition build upon the work of that generation. Rather than seeking to debunk the interpretations of their forebears, these younger historians begin with the assumption that no narrative of American history can be considered complete that ignores the political, social, and cultural experiences of ordinary Americans and that fails to take into account the remarkable diversity that has always characterized American society. But they push this insight in dramatic new directions.

As these essays show, today's leading historians are less interested in developing new subfields or framing either/or dichotomies than in locating intersections and interactions. Categories like race and gender, touchstones of the new social history, are now considered essential to understanding major themes in American development, including the law, diplomacy, and public policy, rather than being limited to relations between blacks and whites or men and women. The distinction between "high" politics and that of ordinary folk has been jettisoned in favor of the study of the broad public sphere, defined so as to encompass many groups who were traditionally excluded from electoral participation yet who engaged in boisterous debates over issues such as economic justice and gender equality. Even national boundaries no longer delimit American history, as evidenced by the number of essays that touch on the history of "borderlands" where various national groups came into contact, as well as on the widespread interest in the global reach of the American experience. An age of globalization seems to demand embedding American history more powerfully than ever in a global framework.

One preoccupation of this new generation of scholars has been to link or reconnect previously fragmented studies of a diverse cast of characters into a new kind of synthesis, one quite different from the old "master narrative" in offering a richer and more complex view of the American past. The chronological essays, for example, devote attention to the importance of elites, established institutions, and public policy, but also place a strong emphasis on how less prominent groups responded to, and affected, constellations of power in the past. Women, Native Americans, workers, slaves, and others appear as important historical actors whose claims contested the shape of power relations. Some essays, like Woody Holton's on the revolutionary era, pointedly depart from the popular fascination with the founding fathers to emphasize the struggles of a broad array of distinct social groups. Others, including Seth Rockman's on the Jacksonian era, Robert Johnston's on Progressive America, and Kim Phillips-Fein's on the years since 1973, emphasize both national authority and the democratic aspirations of less powerful groups.

One theme of the essays that follow is the blurring of previously established scholarly boundaries, as subfields are redefined or abandoned in favor of broader new categories. The new history of capitalism, discussed by Sven Beckert, brings together older subfields such as labor history, business history, and economic history, all within a transnational framework. This new scholarship denaturalizes capitalism by making its emergence a subject of investigation rather than the result of some natural law standing outside of history. Environmental history, an emerging field mapped by Sarah

Phillips, investigates human interactions with the natural universe and the conflicts in politics, society, economics, and the world of ideas over the relationship between human and nonhuman. Diplomatic history, as Erez Manela shows, has been revitalized by incorporating insights from cultural history and benefiting from the "transnational turn." The study of America in the world now includes not simply diplomacy but the activities of nongovernmental actors as well, from performing artists to missionaries and auto salesmen. Mae Ngai charts the recent remaking of immigration history from a field focused on the "assimilation" of European newcomers to a new emphasis on circular worldwide patterns of migration and concepts of cultural diaspora and hybridity. These essays offer vivid examples of what Lawrence Glickman describes as the broader "cultural turn" in historical analysis, which in the past generation has affected virtually every aspect of American history. Cultural historians seek to understand the evolution and hidden power relations within categories—race, class, and so on—that previous scholars took for granted.

Some of the essays cover fields that were ignored in previous editions but have emerged at the forefront of current scholarship. As John McGreevy points out, historians have long neglected the powerful impact of religious faith and religious institutions in the nation's past, but today, thanks in part to the prominent role of religion in contemporary American society, these attract the attention of increasing numbers of historians. Native American history, as Ned Blackhawk delineates, has in recent years become a flourishing enterprise. As Blackhawk shows (and Alan Taylor's essay on the colonial era underscores), attention to the Native American experience profoundly reshapes our understanding of key moments in American history.

"The only obligation we have to history," Oscar Wilde once quipped, "is to rewrite it." There is nothing unusual or sinister in the fact that each generation rewrites history to suit its own needs. Taken together, these essays portray a field characterized by remarkable diversity, vitality, and open-mindedness. They suggest that at its best, the study of history remains a mode of collective self-discovery. This generation is well on the way to fashioning a history of the United States that transcends boundaries rather than reinforcing or reproducing them, that offers a candid appraisal of our own society's strengths and weaknesses while engaging in a mutually illuminating dialogue with the entire world.

Eric Foner
Lisa McGirr

In 1721 in South Carolina, the royal governor received a precious present: a deerskin map conveying a complex world of native peoples and their intricate interconnections. The gift came from Indian chiefs who met Governor Francis Nicholson at Charles Town (now Charleston), the colony's capital and leading seaport. The chiefs represented villages in the Piedmont, where the people spoke a Siouan language. Lumped together by the British (and subsequent historians) as "Catawbas," the people thought of themselves as belonging to a loose confederation of eleven villages named on the map: Casuie, Charra, Nasaw, Nustie, Saxippaha, Succa, Suttirie, Wasmisa, Waterie, Wiapie, and Youchine. The map also locates two more familiar native peoples—the Cherokee and Chickasaw—who had allied with the Catawbas and the British. Rather than represent natives as one, common mass of Indians, the map introduced the governor to a complex network of diverse peoples. Divided into hundreds of linguistically distinct peoples, the natives did not know that they were a common category until named and treated so by the colonial invaders. The Nasaw map warns us to beware of how much nuance we lose when lumping the many native peoples together as "Indians."

By giving the map, the Catawbas sought to educate the new governor to native diplomacy. Rather than depict geographical proportions, the map conveys social and political relationships between peoples, both native and colonial. The thirteen native peoples appear as circles of varying sizes and locations, with the largest and the most central—for the Nasaw—enjoying a pride of place. Asserting a hierarchy of power, the map defines the Nasaw as the pivotal and crucial people in a web of relationships that linked the British colonies of the coast with the Indians of the interior. Take us seriously, and treat us with a special generosity, the Nasaw mapmaker insisted.

A selective depiction of social space, the Nasaw map omits many of the peoples then dwelling between Charles Town, on the east, and the Chickasaws of the Mississippi Valley, to the west. Devoted to the Catawbas and their allies, the map excludes the powerful Creek and Choctaw confederations, who offered rival networks of native power. The map assured Nicholson that the Catawba peoples, and especially the Nasaw, were his special and indispensable friends, who served as his proper conduit into the wider native world of the vast interior. Of course, maps made by other native peoples altered the hierarchy and centrality of villages. In 1723, Nicholson collected a similar map made by the Chickasaws, who gave themselves centrality with strong links to the Choctaw and Cherokee and to the English at Charles Town but with only a marginal place allotted to the Catawbas.

The 1721 Catawba map also represents only two colonial polities: Charles Town appears on the left as a cross-hatching of lines at right angles, while a box named Virginia occupies the lower right-hand corner. The well-rounded natives thought of the newcomers as squares. Living in oval wigwams in circular villages surrounded by palisades, native peoples felt spiritually safest in rounded forms, which reflected the natural cycles of seasons and lives. Their conception of the world as a web of social circles derived from their ancestors who, as recently as the sixteenth century, had sustained the Mississippian culture, which featured many ceremonial mounds. In stark contrast, the Indians identified the colonists with their square and rectangular buildings in towns platted as grids: alien and unnatural forms that seemed ominous.

Rather than reject the strange newcomers, the map represents an Indian bid to incorporate them into a native nexus of diplomacy and trade in the hope that the colonists could learn how to coexist in a shared land. Parallel lines connect both Charles Town and Virginia to the native circles. The lines represented paths of safe conduct for traders and diplomats in a world that could otherwise turn violent. The map coaxed the British to approach the other Catawbas via the Nasaw, who claimed a primacy in trade and diplomacy. To contact the Nustie, for example, good manners demanded sending representatives (and presents of trade goods) first to the Nasaw. Far from accepting subordination to the Virginians or the Carolinians, the Nasaw cast themselves as the brokers of commerce and power in a world dominated by native peoples and conducted in native ways. In this map, Indians hold the center, while the colonists remain marginal.

The self-assurance of the map jars our conventional assumptions about Indians, for we usually narrate colonial history as a relentless and irresistible British drive to dominate and dispossess native peoples. Surely, we assume, natives must have quickly recognized an inferiority dictated by their smaller numbers and inferior technology. We do not expect to find them acting as the self-confident teachers of colonists cast as rather obtuse, but redeemable, students. The map offers an alternative vision of coexistence on native terms, thereby rejecting the colonizers' drive to dispossess native peoples and convert the survivors into Christian menials. Although the governor may not have grasped the intended lesson, the map can teach us more about native thoughts and ways than do the categorical statements of colonizers who lumped all Indians together as immutable primitives meant for eventual conquest.

In addition to the circles, squares, and paths, the map represents three animate beings. First, an especially large human figure wearing a skirt appears to float over the path between Nasaw and Virginia. Lacking a label, she apparently mattered more to the Nasaw mapmaker than to the British copyist. It is tempting to grant her a supernatural power in the minds of the Nasaw. A caption does identify the other, much smaller human figure as "An Indian a Hunting." Evidently male and armed with a musket, he faces an equally small deer. Long a staple of Indian subsistence, hunting deer had become essential to the new and expanding trade with colonists, who valued the hides for tanning to make clothing, especially gloves. By killing deer by the thousands for their hides, the Catawba paid for coveted British manufactures of cloth and metal—including guns and ammunition: goods the natives could not make for themselves. Both by its original material—a deer hide—and by representing a deer-hunting Indian, the map conveyed the trade at the heart of their relationship with the Carolinians.

Finally, in the lower left-hand corner, near Charles Town, the map seems to depict a deployed parachute. But modern eyes trick us into assuming that the English labels define a consistent up and down (or north and south). In fact, the Nasaw intended viewers to circle around the map to view it from every angle without privileging any one side. The apparent parachute is, instead, a ship with a central mast mounted by a pennant and linked by ropes to the deck. In addition to a grid of streets, Charles Town impressed natives as a harbor filled with ships capable of crossing the Atlantic.

The map offers a sophisticated reflection on a changing world where natives killed deer for a transatlantic market while hoping to preserve their traditional spirituality, including a sky woman. The mixed symbols mark the map as at the linkage between two different, but increasingly interpenetrated, networks: the native-made circles and paths of the interior and the Euro-American entrepots of transatlantic commerce.[1]

Two paper copies of the map survive because Governor Nicholson gave them to his patron in England, the Prince of Wales. To render the map meaningful to the prince (and, so, to us), the copyist added the English language labels: translations and representations of the explanations orally conveyed by the chiefs when they delivered their gift. As a cherished curiosity, the copies enabled Nicholson to repay the favors that had promoted his career. That transatlantic career attests to the broad reach of the English empire (which became British in 1707). Born in Yorkshire in 1655, Nicholson was a veteran army officer, who, during the 1670s and 1680s had led troops in Flanders in Europe, Tangier in Morocco, and Boston in New England. He subsequently governed the colonies of New York and Virginia before commanding a failed British bid to conquer French Canada in 1709. A year later Nicholson did capture French Acadia, which became British Nova Scotia, with Nicholson as the first governor. In 1720 he became the first royal governor of South Carolina. Returning to England in 1725, he died in London three years later after a life spent trying to increase the power of an empire along the Atlantic coast of North America.[2]

HISTORIES

Brought together in 1721, the Nasaw mapgivers and the English governor jointly speak to the efforts by historians in recent years to grasp the interplay of the "Atlantic" and "Continental" networks of human movement, trade, diplomacy, and war in North America. "Atlantic historians" examine the complex interplay of Europe, Africa, and the Americas through the transatlantic flows of goods, people, plants, animals, capital, and ideas. American colonization derived from a global expansion of European exploration and commerce beginning in the fifteenth century. In cannonarmed sailing ships, Europeans created the first global nexus of trade by crisscrossing the Atlantic, Indian, and Pacific Oceans. Europe reaped windfall profits from the new global trade, especially in African slaves sent to the Americas to work new plantations devoted to sugar, tobacco, rice, and cacao. Atlantic history is a subset of the larger, global story of European expansion.

During the sixteenth century, the Portuguese led the way around Africa to India, while the Spanish crossed the Atlantic to explore and colonize the Americas. The Spanish took Mexico, to exploit the gold and silver mines, and the largest islands in the Caribbean, where they developed sugar plantations. Coming second, the French concentrated on harvesting the fish of the northern waters and the valuable furs of the northern forests drained by the St. Lawrence River. That left the intervening Atlantic Seaboard for belated exploitation by the English during the early seventeenth century. Disappointed in their hopes for finding precious minerals, the English compensated by creating profitable plantations and farms that attracted thousands of colonists. They also took over a Dutch attempt to create a New Netherland colony in the Hudson and Delaware valleys, between the English colonies in the Chesapeake to the south and New England to the north. In 1707 the English empire became British with the union of Scotland to England under one king and one parliament.

While necessary to assess the colonial era, an Atlantic approach is not sufficient. As Paul Mapp notes, North America was "where an Atlantic world interacted with multiple other worlds." To make sense of colonial North

America we need to combine Atlantic and continental approaches. Mapp and other "continental historians" seek to restore the importance of native peoples to the colonial story. Rather than treat Indians as changing primitives doomed from the start to conquest and assimilation by the colonizers, the continental approach emphasizes the natives' ability to adapt to the newcomers and to compel concessions from them. Instead of lurking beyond the colonies in an ahistorical "wilderness," Indians have come back into the narrative as central and persistent protagonists who helped to shape every colony.

The new combination of Atlantic and continental history challenges the older orthodoxy that treated colonial America as a story of English cultural "seeds" first planted at Jamestown in Virginia in 1607 and at Plymouth in New England in 1620. According to the older view, "American history" began in the east in the English colonies and spread slowly westward, reaching only the Appalachian mountains by independence. In this story, the continent's Indian peoples and Spanish and French colonies seemed relevant only as enemies, as challenges that brought out the best in the English as they remade themselves into Americans.

According to our national origin myth, common English colonists escaped from the rigid customs, social hierarchies, and constrained resources of Europe into an abundant land of both challenge and opportunity. Rising to the challenge, they made the most of their frontier opportunities to prosper by turning the forest into farms. Thereby, they became entrepreneurial and egalitarian individualists who could only be ruled by their own consent. Inevitably, they rebelled against British rule to form an independent and republican union of states destined to expand to the Pacific. Known as "American exceptionalism," this interpretation casts the colonial period simply as an Anglophone preparation for the United States, defined as a uniquely middle-class society and democracy.[3]

American exceptionalism relies on some partial truths. Many British colonists did find more land, greater prosperity, and higher status than they could have achieved by remaining in the mother country. And (save for in the West Indies) British America did lack the aristocrats of the mother country, creating a social vacuum that enabled successful lawyers, merchants, and planters to comprise a colonial elite that favored commercial values. Historians long focused on the political participation of common colonists as voters and legislators in the British colonies. And those scholars scoured colonial events, including the revivals of the Great Awakening, for hints of the coming revolution.

But the traditional story of American uplift obscures the heavy costs of colonization. Especially during the seventeenth century in Virginia and the West Indies, thousands of colonists found only intense labor and early graves owing to diseases and Indian hostility. And those who succeeded bought their good fortune by taking lands from Indians and by exploiting the labor of indentured servants and African slaves. Few Indians and fewer Africans experienced colonial America as a world of attractive new opportunities. Between 1492 and 1776, North America lost population, as diseases and wars killed Indians faster than colonists could replace them. And, during the eighteenth century, most colonial arrivals were African conscripts forcibly carried to a land of slavery, rather than European volunteers seeking a domain of freedom. More than minor aberrations, Indian deaths and the African slaves were fundamental to the success of colonization and the prosperity of the free.

The traditional story also obscures the broad cultural and geographic range of colonial America, which extended far beyond the British colonies of the Atlantic Seaboard. Many native peoples encountered colonizers not as westward-bound Englishmen, but as Spanish heading north from Mexico, as Russians coming eastward from Siberia, or as French probing the Great Lakes and Mississippi River. Each of those colonial ventures interacted in distinctive ways with particular settings and Indians to construct varied Americas—which competed for the trade and alliance of the native peoples in the vast interior between the colonial enclaves.

In recent years, historians have paid greater attention to the broader continent, in general, and to the cultures of native peoples, in particular. These new approaches reveal that colonial societies *did* diverge from their mother countries—but in a more complex and radical manner than imagined within the narrow vision of American uplift for English men. Colonial conditions produced an unprecedented mixing of radically diverse peoples—African, European, and Indian—under stressful circumstances for all. The world had never known such a rapid and intense intermingling of peoples—and of microbes, plants, and animals from different continents. Everyone had to adapt to a new world wrought by those combinations. Thrown together in distant colonies, the diverse peoples from three continents had to find new ways to communicate and to coexist in North America.

The Indians also lived in a new world transformed by the intrusion of diverse newcomers bearing alien diseases, livestock, trade goods, weapons, and Christian beliefs. Ranging across the continent, those processes affected peoples and their environments far from the centers of colonial settlement. Reduced by disease and war, the Siouan peoples of the Carolina Piedmont began to consolidate their villages to form a loose confederation, which eventually became known as the Catawbas. Similar processes of ethnogenesis reshaped native peoples throughout the continent.

Despite the epidemics, the Indians of the interior remained sufficiently numerous and resourceful to slow (and sometimes to reverse) the colonial conquest. For example, on the Great Plains during the eighteenth century, the Indian peoples acquired large herds of horses that endowed them with a new mobility and prowess as buffalo hunters and mounted warriors. Better fed, clothed, and equipped than ever before, the mounted Indians could defy colonial intrusions and even roll back their settlements in Texas and New Mexico.

On the southern Great Plains, the Comanche were the big winners. During the seventeenth century, they had lived as hunter-gatherers in the foothills of the Rocky Mountains. During the early eighteenth century, they traded and raided to obtain horses, which enabled them to push south and east onto the plains to hunt buffalo. By procuring enlarged hunting territories, they improved their bargaining position as traders and their might as warriors. Preying upon the weaker Apaches, the Comanche took women and children captives for trade and for adoption. The many adopted captives and an improved diet of abundant buffalo meat fueled a population growth that starkly contrasted with the demographic decline afflicting most other native peoples. By 1800 the Comanche numbered about 20,000— twice as many as all other native peoples on the southern Great Plains.

Comanche expansion set off a domino effect, as their defeated rivals fled and came into conflict with new neighbors. Reeling from Comanche raids, Apache bands headed westward across the Rio Grande into western New Mexico or they pushed southward deeper into Texas. Many westering Apache refugees found a more secure haven in the canyons of northwest New Mexico. Along their way west, they raided the Pueblo peoples, taking horses, sheep, cattle, and captives. From their captives, the western bands learned weaving, pottery making, and the herding of domestic animals, especially sheep. These composite and increasingly prosperous western bands became known to the Hispanics as the Apache de Navihu—later shortened to Navajo.

Nowhere did the colonizers find a truly empty land free for the taking. However, by the eighteenth century, no natives lived in a primeval isolation from the impact of colonization. Disease epidemics, slave raids, and trade goods spread far beyond the colonies through Indian intermediaries. For example, few Indians lived farther from colonial power than did the Paiutes of the Great Basin: an arid region barely and rarely visited by the Spanish. And yet Ned Blackhawk reveals that hundreds of Paiutes became slaves in eighteenth-century New Mexico. They fell into captivity from raids by their Ute enemies wielding metal weapons obtained in trade from the

Hispanics. That trade in Paiute slaves for manufactured goods sustained a Ute alliance that the Spanish desperately needed to protect New Mexico from other Indians. Such complications prevailed on every frontier as circles and squares overlapped, with both colonizers and natives jostling for an advantage over their rivals.

A hybrid work of cross-cultural translation and explanation, the Nasaw map simplifies to help the governor to grasp a part of the native world. The map focuses on native nations or tribes—the political units most familiar to a European governor. In the process, the map obscures the constituent clans, lineages, and villages—which, in fact, more fundamentally structured the lives of natives. A similar selectivity informs how we write about native peoples, for we remain saddled with a European-derived political vocabulary that casts empires and nations as advanced and complex. In this view, the colonists had coercive state structures with courts, gallows, standing armies, bureaucracies, and hierarchies of command—while Indians did *not*. Unwittingly, we cast their political arrangements as partial, simple, and immature by European standards, for we struggle to grasp their very different modes of complexity, where power derived from the forms and ties of kinship relations. Juliana Barr concludes, "We need to move away from the European constructions of power that are so familiar to us—those grounded in ideas of the state and of racial difference—and try to understand the world as Indians did—organized around kinship-based relationships."

In such a system, native women enjoyed more authority, within delimited realms, than did their colonial counterparts. In most native cultures, women owned the villages, their lands, and the crops—while men hunted, fished, and held the more conspicuous roles as orators, diplomats, and warriors. In that native world, so often at war, women enjoyed a special authority as the makers of peace: cherished and elusive. But they also served as the particular targets of raids to take slaves. In his study of natives and colonists in greater New Mexico, James Brooks reveals that female captives became kin with connections in multiple communities both native and colonial. Some even gained leverage from their cross-cultural expertise, becoming interpreters and brokers of trade and diplomacy between Hispanic settlements and native bands. In a constant cycle of trade and revenge, violence disrupted some families to enrich others as men, both colonial and native, tried to defend their own women and children and to take or buy those of other men. This "captive-exchange system" promoted a violent interdependence rather than peace.

Dependence

Every colonial empire depended on Indian peoples as guides to local plants, landscapes, and animals; as converts for missionary institutions; as trading partners; as slave catchers to retrieve runaway Africans; as raiders to make new slaves of other Indians; and as allies in wars with other empires. Through missions or trade, rival empires tried to build networks of native allies meant to counter those developed by their European rivals. Rather than imposing a pure colonial mastery, those alliances involved the mutual dependence of both colonists and natives. Although natives increasingly relied on European trade goods, they also compelled imperialists to accommodate to native protocols and alliances—often imposing heavy costs and great compromises on imperial visions.

Styling themselves fathers to Indian children, the French longed to dominate all of the natives of the continental interior. But they could never control the dispersed, decentralized, and shifting bands of natives. And in making allies of some, the French had to take on their enemies. Allying with the Algonkin and Huron embroiled the French in debilitating wars with the Haudenosaunee (also known as the "Iroquois") during the seventeenth century. A century later in the Great Lakes country, the Anishinaabe and Illinois manipulated their French allies into attacking the powerful Fox peoples. Brett Rushforth has shown that these native wars compromised the French dream of a universal trade empire engaging every native people in a vast alliance. Native allies repeatedly set limits to French ambitions by giving to them (or obliging them to buy) captives taken from native enemies—including the Fox. Rejecting those captives would wreck the alliance, but accepting them limited the alliance by alienating the raided peoples. The proliferation of enslaved Indians, known as Panis, in Montreal attested to the weakness, rather than to the strength, of the French empire in the Great Lakes watershed.

Savvy imperialists recognized that Indians determined the balance of power within North America. In 1755 an English trader observed,

> The importance of the Indians is now generally known and understood. A Doubt remains not, that the prosperity of our Colonies on the Continent will stand or fall with our Interest and favour among them. While they are our Friends, they are the Cheapest and Strongest Barrier for the Protection of our Settlements; when Enemies, they are capable of ravaging in their method of War, in spite of all we can do, to render those Possessions almost useless.

Despite their reduced numbers, the Indians were skilled guerrilla warriors who dominated the interior passages between the rival colonies. If alienated, the natives could obstruct the advance of their colonial enemy, and their raiders could terrify and destroy outlying settlements.

In regions where the colonizers arrived in relatively small numbers, they had to cultivate native goodwill. In the Great Lakes country during the seventeenth century, the French came by the dozen rather than the thousands. Dependent on Indian trade and protection, the French crafted an alliance based upon mutual accommodations. In the famous phrase of Richard White, the natives and the French found a "middle ground," where neither could dominate the other, so they had to deal with one another as allies.

Indians were even more powerful in eighteenth-century Texas, where colonial missions, presidios, settlements, and trading posts were few, isolated, and vulnerable oases in a native world. In colonial North America, such a native-dominated landscape was more common than, say, Massachusetts or Virginia, with their powerful concentrations of British colonists. Juliana Barr concludes that the native peoples of Texas treated the French and Spanish intruders as "just another collection of bands like themselves." To survive, the newcomers had to offer appealing trade goods, adopt the protocols of native diplomacy, and form kinship ties with the natives through marriage or ritual adoption. Readier to marry native women, the French gained an edge over their Spanish competitors.

Where colonists were few and Indians many, the colonizers tried to convert natives through the agency of missions run by priests. During the seventeenth century, Franciscan friars enjoyed remarkable success in Spanish Florida and New Mexico, founding dozens of missions that attracted thousands of native converts. At the same time, French Jesuits compensated for the small colonial population of Canada by building missions in the St. Lawrence Valley and among the Huron people of the Great Lakes. The inability of traditional shamans to shield their people from the devastating new diseases induced many natives to seek spiritual protection from the missionaries. The ceremonial richness and sacred objects of Catholic worship also impressed the natives, who regarded the crucifixes, rosaries, Agnus Dei medals, and saint's relics as counterparts to the charms and *katsinas* long kept by Indians as sources of spiritual power.

The missions also proffered material and military incentives to entice native peoples. Many Indians coveted European manufactures including metal hoes, knives, fishhooks, hatchets, and cloth blankets—as well as the benefits of domesticated livestock, especially sheep and cattle. Missions often offered a more secure food supply through the seasons than did a traditional, mobile way of life. By converting, native peoples also hoped to secure a military alliance against their enemies. In Canada, the Montagnais, Algonkins, and Hurons sought French help against their Haudenosaunee foes to the south. In Florida, the Spanish promised protection against the Yamasee, Savannah, and Creek peoples to the north of their missions. In New Mexico, the Pueblo peoples needed allies to fend off the nomadic bands of Apache, Navajo, and Comanche who lived in the nearby mountains and Great Plains.

But the conversions were never as complete and irreversible as the priests initially believed, for native peoples regarded Christianity as a supplement, rather than as a substitute, for their traditional beliefs. Natives had long adopted and augmented their spiritual repertoire, clinging to a conceptual framework that regarded supernatural power as diverse and woven into their natural world. They accepted and adapted features of European culture, including Christianity, which they found useful or unavoidable, while privately maintaining their traditional spiritual beliefs. Above all, they tried to preserve a distinct identity and core culture derived from their ancestors. But the missionaries longed to believe that their native converts had forsaken their pagan ways once and for all, without compromise. When suddenly disabused of their illusions, the seventeenth-century missionaries felt betrayed, inflicting excessive punishments that sometimes provoked uprisings. In 1680, for example, the Pueblo peoples revolted, rousting the Spanish from New Mexico. At the end of that century, when the priests and soldiers returned, they behaved with greater circumspection, rebuilding the alliance on terms acceptable to the Pueblos.

Unlike the French and the Spanish, the English rarely developed missions, focusing instead on expanding their farms at Indian expense. Because the Chesapeake and New England colonies attracted many more immigrants than did New Mexico, Florida, and New France *combined*, the English colonists put greater pressure on native lands, provoking more frequent wars. During the late 1640s, a few Puritan clergymen belatedly created mission communities for the natives in New England. In permanent, compact "praying towns" the Indians could be pressured to change their beliefs, behavior, and appearance. By restricting Indians to fixed and limited towns, the Puritans hoped to free up additional lands for colonial settlement. But the Indians had their own reasons for joining the praying towns, which appealed primarily to smaller groups harder hit by disease and the settler intrusion. They saw the praying towns as their last hope for preserving their group identity on a part of their homeland. Indeed, the praying towns bore native names, including "Natick," which meant "my land."

By 1673 the colony of Massachusetts hosted fourteen praying towns with sixteen hundred inhabitants, but most of them collapsed two years later, when other Indians attacked the New English towns. Distrusting the missionized Indians, the colonial authorities sent them to cold and barren islands in Boston harbor, where hundreds died from exposure, malnutrition, and disease. During the spring and summer of 1676, the colonists suppressed the rebels with the help of scouts recruited from the surviving praying-town Indians. Some of the defeated rebels escaped northward to take refuge among the Indians in Canada. Nursing bitter memories, they helped the French to raid New England in subsequent wars between 1689 and 1760.

In Carolina, the English dispensed with missions, relying instead on trade to recruit Indian allies. Compared to their French and Spanish rivals, the Carolina traders offered especially prized trade goods at relatively good prices and on generous credit. Unlike their rivals, the English relied almost exclusively on their economic advantage, rather than on understanding (or converting) the culture of their customers. By offering guns in exchange for deer hides and native captives taken by their allies, the Carolinians secured their own frontier and wreaked havoc on natives who allied with the Spanish in nearby Florida or with the French in Louisiana. Slave raids enabled the Carolina allies to purchase more guns, compounding their military prowess. Raiding also crushed and dispersed rival peoples, opening up their deer-hunting grounds for exploitation by the victors.

The Carolina traders encouraged their allies to attack the Guale, Timucua, and Apalachee Indians who lived in the Spanish missions of Florida. Poorly armed by the Spanish, the mission Indians proved easy pickings for slave raids. Between 1704 and 1706 the Creek, Savannah, and Yamasee raiders destroyed thirty-two native villages and their missions, inflicting horrific casualties and enslaving about ten thousand people. The Carolina gun and slave trade had triumphed over the Spanish mission system as an instrument of colonial influence.

After the destruction of the Florida missions, potential captives became scarcer, and the raiders fell into arrears on their debts owed to the Carolina traders. In 1715 the Yamasees and the Cawtawbas sought to escape their debts by killing traders and attacking the Carolina settlements, killing about 400 and driving hundreds of refugees into Charles Town. But the Indian rebels lost momentum as they ran low on guns and gunpowder. They had counted on a continued supply from the British traders in Virginia, who competed with their counterparts in the Carolinas. Although the traders and leaders of Carolina and Virginia bickered almost constantly, during an Indian war their national and racial consciousness united them as English and white. Putting

                                                    American History Now

aside their rivalries, the Virginians assisted the Carolinians with weapons and troops and with an embargo on the trade in guns and gunpowder to the rebels. Aided by Tuscarora and Cherokee allies, the Carolinians forced the Catawbas to make peace and to help them subdue and enslave the Yamasees.

Threatened by the slave raids of Carolina's allies, the Indians in the Mississippi Valley sought an alliance with the French who founded Louisiana in 1699. From Carolina's success and Florida's failure, the French concluded that a commerce in guns better secured native support than did missionaries, so, in Louisiana, the French made gun trade, rather than missions, their priority in Indian relations. By uniting and arming the Mississippi Valley peoples, the French sought to stabilize them as enduring allies to keep the British away from Louisiana. But the French could not match the quantity, quality, and price of British manufactures, so they had to rely on bestowing trade goods as government-funded presents. Lacking the means to satisfy all the Indian nations on their periphery, the French had to settle for allying primarily with the numerous Choctaws. Unable also to supply the Chickasaws, the French accepted them as enemies who traded with the Carolinians. Indeed, during the 1720s the French encouraged the Choctaws to raid the Chickasaws for slaves.

The vast colony of Louisiana became two very different landscapes: a small plantation core around New Orleans, where settlers prevailed, and an immense hinterland dominated by Indians. In the interior, the French held only a few small and scattered forts hostage to the goodwill of the surrounding natives. French officials claimed that they had a particular gift for understanding and conciliating Indians, but their claim was only half true, for they conducted contrasting policies in Louisiana. In the hinterland, the French made a virtue of their weakness by cultivating some natives as their cherished allies (while treating others as necessary enemies). But, in the colony's core, where the colonists and their slaves were more numerous, the French treated natives as callously as did any other colonizers.

The Louisianans also worked to keep Indians and Africans apart lest they unite to destroy the plantations. To sow antipathies, the French conspicuously employed some trusted blacks in their militias sent to fight the Indians. A few particularly courageous and resourceful black soldiers won their freedom as a reward meant to inspire the exertions of their enslaved comrades. However, colonial leaders rewarded the Choctaw to hunt down runaway slaves and to punish rebel slaves by burning them to death. But the Louisiana elite also distrusted their own lower-class whites as little better, and sometimes worse, than Indians or enslaved Africans. Regarded as felons and vagrants, the common settlers and soldiers of Louisiana found that a white skin brought them far less privilege than it did to the common people of Carolina. In sum, the French relied on blacks and natives to control lower-class whites just as they employed Africans and Indians against one another.

That Louisiana balancing act contrasted with the British colonial tendency toward a greater formal equality and liberty for all white men, as they increasingly equated freedom with the white race and their property rights over Africans. Relative to the French, the British colonists enjoyed greater liberties from, and voice within, their government—and more shared power over slaves. As the British Americans grew even more numerous, prosperous, and confident, they developed their white racial solidarity and popular government.

Although commercially weaker than the British of Carolina, the French of Louisiana had the edge as Indian traders over the Spanish of New Mexico. The workshops in Spain were less productive, Spanish shipping more expensive, and trade more strictly regulated and heavily taxed by officials. Consequently, Spanish goods were more expensive and of lower quality than those offered by their French and British competitors. During the eighteenth century, that discrepancy had ominous consequences for security along the vast northern frontier of New Spain.

Although allies elsewhere, the French and Spanish became bitter rivals for sway with the native peoples in the immense Great Plains between French Louisiana and Hispanic New Mexico. Lacking guns to trade to the natives, the Spanish lost a trade war to the more accommodating French, who understood that trade bought influence and redirected Indian warfare against other natives in a rival trade orbit. During the 1710s and 1720s, the French-armed Comanche, Pawnee, and Wichitas raided the poorly armed villages of Apaches and Pueblos allied to the Spanish. The victorious raiders took captives to sell to the French traders in payment for more guns and ammunition. When facing east, the French opposed the English slave trade based in Carolina, but when facing west, the French encouraged their Great Plains clients to prey on poorly armed natives allied with the Spanish.

Beleaguered by French-armed raiders, the Spanish reformed their frontier policy during the late eighteenth century. Deemphasizing missions, the frontier officials sought to woo some Indian allies with presents of trade goods: the Louisiana French model. Partial success reduced the pressure on New Mexico, which had begun modestly, to prosper and grow, doubling its population from ninety-six hundred in 1765 to twenty thousand by 1800.

While New Mexico became more secure, the Spanish felt newly threatened on their northwestern flank, along the Pacific coast of California. During the mid-1760s, the Spanish belatedly learned of Russian explorers and fur traders active in the Aleutian Islands and along the southern coast of Alaska. The Spanish dreaded a Russian plot to strike south along the Pacific coast to attack precious Mexico. Spanish officials also exaggerated reports that British fur traders had crossed the northern Great Plains and the Rocky Mountains to approach the Pacific. The royal inspector general in New Spain, Jose de Galvez, concluded, "There is no doubt that in any case we have the English very close to our towns of New Mexico, and not very far from the west coast of this continent."

In 1768, to secure Mexico against both the Russian and the British phantoms, Galvez sent a small military expedition to occupy the Alta California coast with a system of forts, known as presidios, supported by missions run by Franciscan priests. For want of sufficient colonists, the Spanish revived in California a mission system that they had downplayed elsewhere as retrograde. By 1784, Alta California had only two towns, four presidios, and nine missions. The approximately nine hundred Hispanic colonists were stretched thin along a five-hundred-mile long coast from San Francisco to San Diego and scattered among thousands of Indians—twenty thousand of whom had joined the missions. As in other mission systems, the California Indians sought to preserve as much autonomy and land as possible "within an increasingly confining colonial order" (in the words of Steven Hackel).

ENDS

While the Russians and Spanish jockeyed for an edge in the northwest, the British and the French escalated their warfare in the continent's northeastern quarter. Between 1689 and 1763, their empires waged four wideranging wars. Initially, the French and British concentrated their fighting in Europe, treating the colonies as a mere sideshow. That policy changed in the ultimate colonial conflict, the Seven Years War, which began in 1754, when the British invested men and money as never before to conquer New France.

Although divided into many tribes and subdivided into hundreds of villages, the Indian peoples of the Great Lakes and Ohio Valley shared a broad interest in prolonging their strategic middle position between the French and the British colonies. By exploiting the competition between the traders and officials of rival empires, the Indians sought favorable prices and abundant presents from both. By the 1750s, however, the chiefs felt alarmed by the growing British colonial population, which threatened to break through the Appalachian mountains into the continental interior. In 1754 the 1.5 million British colonists (and slaves) greatly outnumbered the seventy thousand French in North America.

Superior numbers emboldened the British to treat the Indians more arrogantly than did the French. British colonial officials could do little to stop their settlers from stealing Indian lands and taking Indian lives. The French, however, relied on Indian allies to hold the interior against encroaching British settlers, traders, and soldiers. Lightly built and garrisoned, the French forts depended on the natives for protection and paid for it with presents and mediation. In general, the Indians of the Great Lakes and Ohio Valley welcomed the French forts as assets instead of resenting them as threats. In sum, by 1750 the natives faced a greater threat from the numerous and aggressive British than from the few and more generous French.

In 1754 imperial war resumed between the French and the British, with North America as the prime stakes. During the early years of that war, Indian allies helped the French to repel British attacks. But that native support softened as the British exploited their great countervailing advantage in offering superior trade goods in abundant quantities and at cheaper prices. The powerful British navy compounded that trade advantage by controlling the sea lanes and destroying French merchant shipping. Running out of trade goods, the colonial French could not supply their Indian allies, inducing many to make peace with the British. The defection of their native allies exposed Canada to a British invasion, which conquered Louisbourg in 1758, Quebec in 1759, and Montreal in 1760. Three years later the defeated French made a peace treaty that awarded Canada, the Great Lakes Country, and the Ohio Valley to the triumphant British.

British success threatened the Indian peoples of the interior, for they depended upon playing off rival empires to maintain their own autonomy. Deprived of a French counterweight, the British Empire could sweep settlements deep into the continent, pushing the Indians aside and transforming their land into farms and towns. But the Indians taught the British a bloody lesson by rebelling in 1763 to destroy most of the forts around the Great Lakes. To cut their losses, the British resumed giving presents to the Indians and tried to control the settler invasion of the Ohio Valley.

That British rapprochement with the Indians threatened colonial allegiance to the empire. After making such a major investment of money and lives to conquer Canada, the British were not about to resume their former policy of benign neglect. During the 1760s, Parliament and the Crown worked to tighten imperial management in an enlarged domain that threatened to spin out of control. Concluding that the empire was too weak and the colonists too insubordinate, the British tightened enforcement of the trade laws, kept a permanent garrison in North America, and imposed new taxes to pay for it. That shift in imperial policy shocked the colonial leaders, who felt a new confidence in their ability to defy the British Empire—if necessary—and to conquer and develop the continent for their own purposes.

While securing the liberty of white men, their revolution would also build their own empire within the continent. By expanding westward during the following century, the new United States would dominate the continent by conquering Hispanics as well as the Indians. From their colonial forebears, the citizens of the United States inherited an expansionist zeal driven by a defensive dread. During the wars of the 1750s and 1760s, the diverse British colonists had crafted a new, shared identity as "white people" and Americans by defining themselves against their Indian enemies. Particularly in the Middle Colonies of New York, Pennsylvania, and New Jersey, the German, Dutch, English, Welsh, Scots, and Irish immigrants set aside their old ethnic and religious differences by focusing on their new shared animosity for Indians. According to Peter Silver, the colonists imagined themselves as the innocent victims of brutal savages preying especially on women and children. By indulging in lurid depictions of scalping and torture, colonial men exhorted one another to live up to their patriarchal ideals by taking vengeance on native warriors. And they cast as a race traitor anyone who defended Indians or faulted their killers. By downplaying denominational and ethnic difference, the rhetoric created an American nationalism that emphasized white and male supremacy as essential to defend their families.

Lumped together as a hostile enemy, Indians began to construct their own collective identity as "red people" who should unite against the invaders. In a process that paralleled the emerging racial identity of the white colonists, the most visionary Indians sought to submerge their traditional tribal enmities in a new pan-Indian confederation. In the Great Lakes country and Ohio Valley, that vision lay behind the native victory over the British in "Pontiac's Rebellion" of the mid-1760s. During the revolution and into the 1790s, those natives repeatedly defeated the forces of the United States. Thereafter, however, the new nation crushed the pan-Indian resistance, opening the continent up to American conquest.

Even in eventual defeat, the Indian enemy exercised a powerful hold over the cultural imagination of Americans, affecting even the domestic life of colonial women. In an innovative examination of cloth and cloth making, the historian Laurel Thatcher Ulrich demonstrates how the labor of white women helped to domesticate the lands taken from Indians: "cloth literally transformed the landscape as Algonkian beaver passed into the hands of English felt-makers and English sheep began to graze on American meadows." But Ulrich also refutes the mythic insistence that New England's Indians had vanished. She closely analyzes the nineteenth-century Indian baskets collected by the mythmakers, who remained oblivious to their testimony that the natives adapted and persisted long after their supposed disappearance. Often misinterpreted as timeless and primeval survivals, those baskets, in fact, employed new materials, techniques, and designs to appeal to nonnative consumers. In recent years, historians have broken with the essentialist notion of Indians as noble primitives capable of change only as a form of decay. Rejecting that ahistorical fantasy, historians now define "Indianness" as an adaptability that interweaves tradition with innovation in a struggle for cultural survival in a transformed land.

Employing war, treaties, and myths, the colonists worked to pin natives down within delimited reservations surrounded by settlements in a long process that triumphed during the nineteenth century. Reservations both enabled and depended upon a surrounding thicket of the private property lines for thousands of farms. A colony reaped allegiance from the specula-tors and settlers whose property depended on the land titles issued by the government and defended by its courts and militia. Energized by that grid of private property, settlers made farms by clearing the forest, depleting the wild animals, and fencing new fields. That environmental transformation alienated the land from the native peoples, who had relied on a widerang-ing mix of hunting, fishing, and horticulture. In sum, the making of private landholdings and the defining of Indian reservations were reciprocal pro-cesses. The colonial surveyors created a landscape of rectilinear tracts that obscures the native world of circles beneath and before.

Heirs to a world of square buildings and properties, we need to recall the very different cultural landscape of colonial America, where natives hoped to integrate the newcomers into a network of circles and paths. To under-stand the true sweep of colonial America and the pivotal importance of native peoples, multiply by a thousand the circles and the relational paths of the Nasaw map. Extend that array across the continent with links to Brit-ish squares up and down the Atlantic seaboard; Spanish squares in Florida, Texas, New Mexico, and California; French squares in the Mississippi and St. Lawrence watersheds; and even Russian squares in the far northwest along the Aleutian Islands and the Alaska coast. That dense and complex picture belies the imperial fantasies of textbook maps where the claims of vast European empires cover the continent, prematurely submerging the many native peoples. Indeed, it took four centuries of trial and error, strug-gle and setback for Euroamericans to dominate the continent. During the long colonial era, the natives of the vast interior could oblige sojourning traders and soldiers to play by the rules of native diplomacy. Circles were not squares, but both had to share paths between them.

NOTES

1. White, "Nationalization of Nature," 978–979, urges attention to the overlap and connections of different scales of analysis: local, regional, national, and global.

2. Webb, "Strange Career." Although the deerskin original has long rotted away, two paper copies, with English labels, survive in British archives: the British Museum in London and the National Archives of the United Kingdom (in Kew).

3. For critiques, see Chaplin, "Expansion and Exceptionalism"; Tyrrell, "American Exceptionalism"; Bender, *Nation among Nations*, 15–60.

BIBLIOGRAPHY

The scholarly literature on colonial North America is so rich, diverse, and voluminous that the following bibliography offers only a selection, primarily recent works or relevant to the theme of this chapter.

Adelman, Jeremy, and Stephen A. Aron. "From Borderlands to Borders: Empires, Nation-States, and the Peoples in Between in North American History." *American Historical Review* 104 (1999): 814–841.

Anderson, Fred. *Crucible of War: The Seven Years' War and the Fate of Empire in British North America, 1754–1766*. New York: Knopf, 2000.

Axtell, James. *The Invasion Within: The Contest of Cultures in Colonial North America*. New York: Oxford University Press, 1985.

———. *The Indians' New South: Cultural Change in the Colonial Southeast*. Baton Rouge: Louisiana State University Press, 1997.

Barr, Juliana, *Peace Came in the Form of a Woman: Indians and Spaniards in the Texas Borderlands*. Chapel Hill: University of North Carolina Press, 2007.

Bender, Thomas. *A Nation among Nations*. New York: Hill and Wang, 2006.

Berlin, Ira. *Many Thousands Gone: The First Two Centuries of Slavery in North America*. Cambridge, MA: Harvard University Press, 1998.

Blackhawk, Ned. *Violence over the Land: Indians and Empires in the Early American West*. Cambridge, MA: Harvard University Press, 2006.

Bohaker, Heidi. "Nindoodemag: The Significance of Algonquian Kinship Networks in Eastern Great Lakes Region, 1600–1701." *William and Mary Quarterly*, 3rd. ser., 63 (2006): 23–52.

Braund, Kathryn E. Holland. *Deerskins and Duffels: The Creek Indian Trade with Anglo-America, 1685–1815*. Lincoln: University of Nebraska Press, 1993.

Brooks, James F. *Captives and Cousins: Slavery, Kinship, and Community in the Southwest Borderlands*. Chapel Hill: University of North Carolina Press, 2002.

Calloway, Colin G., ed. *After King Philip's War: Presence and Persistence in Indian New England*. Hanover, NH: University Press of New England, 1997.

———. *One Vast Winter Count: The Native American West before Lewis and Clark*. Lincoln: University of Nebraska Press, 2003.

Canny, Nicholas, and Anthony Pagden, eds. *Colonial Identity in the Atlantic World, 1500–1800*. Princeton, NJ: Princeton University Press, 1987.

Cayton, Andrew R. L., and Fredrika J. Teute, eds. *Contact Points: American Frontiers from the Mohawk Valley to the Mississippi, 1750–1830*. Chapel Hill: University of North Carolina Press, 1998.

Chaplin, Joyce. "Expansion and Exceptionalism in Early American History." *Journal of American History* 89 (2003): 1431–1455.

Coclanis, Peter A. "Atlantic World or Atlantic/World?" *William and Mary Quarterly*, 3rd ser., 63 (2006): 725–742.

Crosby, Alfred W., Jr. *The Columbian Exchange: Biological and Cultural Consequences of 1492*. Norman: University of Oklahoma Press, 1972.

———. *Ecological Imperialism: The Biological Expansion of Europe, 900–1900*. New York: Cambridge University Press, 1986.

Daniels, Christine, and Michael V. Kennedy, eds. *Negotiated Empires: Centers and Peripheries in the Americas, 1500–1820*, 1–14. New York: Routledge, 2002.

Delage, Denys. *Bitter Feast: Amerindians and Europeans in Northeastern North America, 1600–1664*. Vancouver: University of British Columbia Press, 1993.

Deloria, Philip. *Indians in Unexpected Places*. Lawrence: University Press of Kansas, 2004.

Dowd, Gregory Evans. *A Spirited Resistance: The North American Indian Struggle for Unity, 1745–1815*. Baltimore: Johns Hopkins University Press, 1992.

DuVal, Kathleen. *The Native Ground: Indians and Colonists in the Heart of the Continent*. Philadelphia: University of Pennsylvania Press, 2006.

Fenn, Elizabeth Anne. *Pox Americana: The Great Smallpox Epidemic of 1775–1782*. New York: Hill and Wang, 2001.

Gallay, Alan. *The Indian Slave Trade: The Rise of the English Empire in the American South, 1670–1717*. New Haven, CT: Yale University Press, 2002.

Games, Alison. "Beyond the Atlantic: English Globetrotters and Transoceanic Connections." *William and Mary Quarterly*, 3rd. ser., 63 (2006): 675–692.

Greer, Allan. *Mohawk Saint: Catherine Tekakwitha and the Jesuits*. New York: Oxford University Press, 2005.

Griffin, Patrick, *American Leviathan: Empire, Nation, and Revolutionary Frontier*. New York: Hill and Wang, 2007.

Gutierrez, Ramon A. *When Jesus Came, the Corn Mothers Went Away: Marriage, Sexuality, and Power in New Mexico, 1500–1846*. Stanford, CA: Stanford University Press, 1991.

Hackel, Steven W., ed. *Alta California: Peoples in Motion, Identities in Formation, 1769–1850*. Berkeley: University of California Press, 2010.

————. *Children of Coyote, Missionaries of Saint Francis: Indian-Spanish Relations in Colonial California, 1769–1850*. Chapel Hill: University of North Carolina Press, 2005.

Hall, Gwendolyn Midlo. *Africans in Colonial Louisiana: The Development of Afro-Creole Culture in the Eighteenth Century*. Baton Rouge: Louisiana State University Press, 1995.

Hamalainen, Pekka. *The Comanche Empire*. New Haven, CT: Yale University Press, 2008.

Hijiya, James. "Why the West Is Lost." *William and Mary Quarterly*, 3rd. ser., 51(1994): 276–292.

Hinderaker, Eric. *Elusive Empires: Constructing Colonialism in the Ohio Valley, 1673–1800*. New York: Cambridge University Press, 1997.

————. *The Two Hendricks: Unraveling a Mohawk Mystery*. Cambridge, MA: Harvard University Press, 2010.

Hinderaker, Eric, and Peter C. Mancall. *At the Edge of Empire: The Backcountry in British North America*. Baltimore: Johns Hopkins University Press, 2003.

Horn, James. *Adapting to a New World: English Society in the Seventeenth-Century Chesapeake*. Chapel Hill: University of North Carolina Press, 1994.

Hudson, Charles, and Carmen Chaves Tesser, eds. *The Forgotten Centuries: Indians and Europeans in the American South, 1521–1704*. Athens: University of Georgia Press, 1994.

Jacobs, Wilbur R., ed. *Indians of the Southern Colonial Frontier: The Edmond Atkin Report and Plan of 1755*. Columbia: University of South Carolina Press, 1954.

Knaut, Andrew L. *The Pueblo Revolt of 1680: Conquest and Resistance in Seventeenth-Century New Mexico*. Norman: University of Oklahoma Press, 1997.

Lepore, Jill. *The Name of War: King Philip's War and the Origins of American Identity*. New York: Knopf, 1998.

Liss, Peggy. *Atlantic Empires: The Network of Trade and Revolution, 1713–1826*. Baltimore: Johns Hopkins University Press, 1983.

Lockhart, James, ed. *Of Things of the Indies: Essays Old and New in Early American History*. Stanford, CA: Stanford University Press, 1999.

Mapp, Paul W. "Atlantic History from Imperial, Continental, and Pacific Perspectives." *William and Mary Quarterly*, 3rd. ser., 63 (2006): 713–724. (Quote on p. 718.)

Merrell, James. *The Indians' New World: Catawbas and Their Neighbors from European Contact through the Era of Removal*. Chapel Hill: University of North Carolina Press, 1989).

———. *Into the American Woods: Negotiators on the Pennsylvania Frontier*. New York: W. W. Norton, 1999.

Merritt, Jane T. *At the Crossroads: Indians and Empires on a Mid-Atlantic Frontier, 1700–1763*. Chapel Hill: University of North Carolina Press, 2003.

Murrin, John M. "Beneficiaries of Catastrophe: The English Colonies in America." In Eric Foner, ed., *The New American History*, 3–30. Philadelphia: Temple University Press, 1997.

Nobles, Gregory H. *American Frontiers: Cultural Encounters and Continental Conquest*. New York: Hill and Wang, 1997.

O'Brien, Jean M. *Dispossession by Degrees: Indian Land and Identity in Natick, Massachusetts, 1650–1790*. New York: Cambridge University Press, 1997.

Pestana, Carla Gardina. *The English Atlantic in an Age of Revolution, 1640–1661*. Cambridge, MA: Harvard University Press, 2004.

Piker, Joshua. *Okfuskee: A Creek Indian Town in Colonial America*. Cambridge, MA: Harvard University Press, 2004.

Pulsipher, Jenny Hale. *Subjects unto the Same King: Indians, English, and the Contest for Authority in Colonial New England*. Philadelphia: University of Pennsylvania Press, 2005.

Resendez, Andres. *Changing National Identities at the Frontier: Texas and New Mexico, 1800–1850*. New York: Cambridge University Press, 2005.

Richter, Daniel K. *Facing East from Indian Country: A Native History of Early America*. Cambridge, MA: Harvard University Press, 2001.

Rushforth, Brett. "'A Little Flesh We Offer You': The Origins of Indian Slavery in New France." *William and Mary Quarterly*, 3rd. ser., 60 (2003): 777–808.

———. "Slavery, the Fox Wars, and the Limits of Alliance." *William and Mary Quarterly*, 3rd ser., 63 (2006): 53–80.

Salisbury, Neal. *Manitou and Providence: Indians, Europeans, and the Making of New England, 1500–1643*. New York: Oxford University Press, 1982.

Saunt, Claudio, "Go West: Mapping Early American Historiography," *William and Mary Quarterly*, 3rd ser., 65 (2008): 745–778.

Seed, Patricia. *Ceremonies of Possession in Europe's Conquest of the New World, 1492–1640*. New York: Cambridge University Press, 1995.

Shoemaker, Nancy, ed. *Negotiators of Change: Historical Perspectives on Native American Women*. New York: Routledge, 1995.

———. *A Strange Likeness: Becoming Red and White in Eighteenth-Century North America*. New York: Oxford University Press, 2004.

Silver, Peter. *Our Savage Neighbors: How Indian War Transformed Early America*. New York: W. W. Norton, 2008.

Silverman, David J. *Faith and Boundaries: Colonists, Christianity, and Community among the Wampanoag Indians of Martha's Vineyard, 1600–1871*. New York: Cambridge University Press, 2005.

Sleeper-Smith, Susan. *Indian Women and French Men: Rethinking Cultural Encounter in the Western Great Lakes*. Amherst: University of Massachusetts Press, 2001.

Smith, Barbara Sweetland, and Redmond J. Barnett, eds. *Russian America: The Forgotten Frontier*. Tacoma: Washington State Historical Society, 1990.

Steele, Ian K. *The English Atlantic, 1675–1740: An Exploration of Communication and Community*. New York: Oxford University Press, 1986.

———. *Warpaths: Invasions of North America*. New York: Oxford University Press, 1994.

Sweet, John Wood. *Bodies Politic: Negotiating Race in the American North, 1730–1830*. Baltimore: Johns Hopkins University Press, 2003.

Taylor, Alan. *American Colonies*. New York: Viking/Penguin, 2001.

———. *The Divided Ground: Indians, Settlers, and the Northern Borderland of the American Revolution*. New York: Knopf, 2006.

Thornton, John. *Africa and Africans in the Making of the Atlantic World, 1400–1680*. New York: Cambridge University Press, 1992.

Tyrrell, Ian. "American Exceptionalism in an Age of International History." *American Historical Review* 96 (1991): 1031–1055.

Ulrich, Laurel Thatcher. *The Age of Homespun: Objects and Stories in the Creation of an American Myth*. New York: Knopf, 2001.

Usner, Daniel H., Jr. *Indians, Settlers, and Slaves in a Frontier Exchange Economy: The Lower Mississippi Valley before 1783*. Chapel Hill: University of North Carolina Press, 1992.

Vigil, Ralph H., Frances W. Kaye, and John R. Wunder, eds. *Spain and the Plains: Myths and Realities of Spanish Exploration and Settlement on the Great Plains*. Niwot: University Press of Colorado, 1994.

Warhus, Mark. *Another America: Native Maps and the History of Our Land*. New York: St. Martin's Press, 1997.

Waselkov, Gregory A. "Indian Maps of the Colonial Southeast." In Peter H. Wood, Gregory A. Waselkov, and M. Thomas Hatley, eds., *Powhatan's Mantle: Indians in the Colonial Southeast, 320–324*. Lincoln: University of Nebraska Press, 1989.

Webb, Stephen S. "The Strange Career of Francis Nicholson." *William and Mary Quarterly*, 3rd. ser., 23 (1966): 513–548.

Weber, David J. *Barbaros: Spaniards and their Savages in the Age of Enlightenment*. New Haven, CT: Yale University Press, 2005.

———. *The Spanish Frontier in North America*. New Haven, CT: Yale University Press, 1992.

West, Elliott. *The Way to the West: Essays on the Central Plains*. Albuquereque: University of New Mexico Press, 1995.

White, Richard. *The Middle Ground: Indians, Empires, and Republics in the Great Lakes Region, 1650–1815*. New York: Cambridge University Press, 1991.

———. "The Nationalization of Nature." *Journal of American History* 86 (1999): 976–986.

———. *Roots of Dependency: Subsistence, Environment, and Social Change among the Choctaws, Pawnees, and Navajos*. Lincoln: University of Nebraska Press, 1983.

Wood, Betty. *The Origins of American Slavery: Freedom and Bondage in the English Colonies*. New York: Hill and Wang, 1997.

Wood, Gordon S. *The Radicalism of the American Revolution*. New York: Knopf, 1992.